The
Government
of
VIRGINIA

In the Seventeenth Century

By
Thomas J. Wertenbaker

CLEARFIELD

Originally published as
Jamestown 350th Anniversary Historical Booklet, Number 16
Williamsburg, Virginia, 1957

Copyright © 1957
Virginia 350th Anniversary Celebration Corporation
Williamsburg, Virginia
All Rights Reserved

Reprinted for Clearfield Company by
Genealogical Publishing Company
Baltimore, Maryland
1994, 2012

ISBN 978-0-8063-4513-0

Made in the United States of America

The Government of Virginia in the Seventeenth Century

It was in May 1607 that three little vessels, the *Susan Constant*, the *Discovery*, and the *Godspeed*, entered the Chesapeake Bay. The men who crowded against the rails to view the shores of a strange new world were delighted with the fair meadows, made colorful by the many kinds of flowers, and with the streams of fresh water. Entering the mouth of a great river, which they called the James in honor of their King, they made their way up into the country. At last, finding a peninsula in the river, they came ashore, landed their stores, and set to work building houses, and erecting palisaded fortifications. This place they called Jamestown. It was the first successful beachhead of English civilization on the continent of North America.

One wonders whether there came to the little band who came thus into the unknown wilderness any vision of the millions who were to follow in their wake, of the great cities, the prosperous farms, the rich mines, the vast highways that would one day cover the country. Did they wonder what type of government Englishmen would live under here? Would America become a land of despotism, or would men be free? In the charter of 1606, granted by King James I to the Virginia Company of London, it was promised that they should "enjoy all the liberties, franchises and immunities" of Englishmen, "as if they had been abiding" in England. Many years later Francis Moryson and Thomas Ludwell, agents for the colony of Virginia in England, wrote: "If His Majesty plant a colony of Englishmen by their own consent, or permit one to be founded ... such planters and their heirs ought by law to enjoy in such plantation the same liberties and privileges as Englishmen in England, such

1

plantation being but in nature of an extension or dilation of the realm of England."

So Virginians claimed as their birthright a voice in the government through representatives of their own choosing; the enjoyment of the habeas corpus and jury trial; freedom from punishment save by due process of law; and, above all, the right to be taxed only by their own consent. Moryson and Ludwell said they conceived it "to be the right of the Virginians, as well as all other Englishmen, . . . not to be taxed but by their consent, expressed by their representatives." Upon this right, which was not seriously challenged in Virginia until the passage of the Stamp Act, the development of self-government was chiefly based. As it was the control of the purse by the Commons which made that body supreme in England, so the power of the purse made the House of Burgesses the controlling power in the colony.

But, when Englishmen first came to America, liberty in England still hung in the balance. King James I had little sympathy with the cry for popular rights. He thought of himself as the father of his people. His function was to rule, to rule wisely and well, but if necessary sternly. The people, for their part, like good children should obey. If they did not, they were scolded and called undutiful. To question the King's authority was not only illegal, but wicked.

It remained to be seen which conception would prevail in the colony. Would the Virginians of the future consent to be governed by a King residing three thousand miles away, who knew little of their needs and problems, and probably cared less? Or would they assert their right to govern themselves? The answer depended in part on events in England. If absolutism were established there, absolutism would follow in the colony; if the rule of Parliament prevailed, the House of Burgesses would become the governing body in Virginia. So events in the colony during the seventeenth century reflected the great movements in England—the First Stuart Despotism, the Civil War and Commonwealth, the Restoration, the Second Stuart Despotism, and the Glorious Revolution.

But there were forces in America, different from any in England, which tended toward democracy. America was a frontier. The open spaces bred a spirit of independence, for in them men had of necessity to be self-reliant. When one had with his own hands cleared a space in the forest, laid out his crop of tobacco and Indian corn, built his little cabin, sunk his own well, fenced in a bit of land for his cattle, one was in no humor to be told what to do or not do by a distant monarch.

The history of America from the earliest days to the present has been marked by the rise of poor men to a condition of wellbeing, the creation of a vast, prosperous, and intelligent middle class. And it is this, more than all our laws, more even than our Constitution, which makes us a democratic people. During the larger part of the seventeenth century the poor man, even though he might have come to Virginia as an indentured worker, had every opportunity to rise. As a result there developed a vigorous, independent yeomanry, and though many poor planters were ruined by the early operation of the Navigation Acts, and many more by the introduction of slaves in large numbers, the class survived throughout the colonial period. And it would be difficult to exaggerate their influence in winning self-government for Virginia.

But the outlook at first was dark. When King James I gave his assent to the founding of Virginia, it was not his intention to transplant liberal institutions to the New World. His own Parliament in England gave him trouble enough; he did not wish to set up little colonial Assemblies to take their cue from it to resist and thwart him. So, when in 1606, he granted a charter to the Virginia Company of London, he was careful to keep the control of the proposed colony in his own hands.

The charter provided for a Council, appointed by the King and directly responsible to him, who were to be resident in Eng-

3

land, and to whom was assigned the management of the colony. This body was to name another Council, which was to live in Virginia, and, subject to the laws and instructions prescribed by the King, administer its affairs. There was no mention of a representative body. In practice the isolation of the settlement operated to make the Council in Virginia largely independent of both King and Company, and they at once assumed administrative, legislative, and judicial powers.

As a temporary expedient the plan might have worked well had there been a wiser choice of the members of the Virginia Council. But they proved a quarrelsome set of men, more interested in furthering each his own authority than the good of the colony. Their meetings were stormy. At the first landing there were seven Councillors, but two were soon deposed by their colleagues, one died, and a fourth, Captain Newport, commander of the little fleet, left for England. The three who were left seem to have ruled with a harsh hand. Edward Wingfield, one of the expelled members, said that were their "whipping, lawing, beating, and hanging" known in England, it would turn many against the colony. Finally, with the drowning of two new Councillors and the death by sickness of another, Captain John Smith alone remained, and for several months was the sole ruler of the colony.

When it became obvious to the London Company that the original plan of government had proved a failure, they obtained from the King a new charter, empowering them to change it. So they abolished the Virginia Council and entrusted the control of the colony to an all-powerful Governor. It was a case of sending a stork to be king of the frogs. Fortunately the first selection, Thomas Lord De La Warr, was a good one. Upon his arrival peace and prosperity seemed to come to the little colony. The people, forgetting their quarrels, set to work to build houses, repair the fort, plant crops, and restore the little church.

Then misfortune struck again. De La Warr fell ill. When he

had suffered successively with what seems to have been malaria, dysentery, gout, and scurvy, he set sail for the West Indies in the hope of recovering his health. The command of the colony then was taken over by Sir Thomas Gates as De La Warr's deputy.

Previously Gates had posted in the church certain laws, orders, and instructions that were more fit for a penal colony than for free Englishmen. No one should give "any disgraceful words" upon pain of "being tied head and feet together" every night for a month. To kill any of the livestock was punishable with death. The good wife who did her washing too close to the well might pay for it with lashes on her back.

Under De La Warr and Gates these laws seem not to have been enforced, but under Sir Thomas Dale, who took over the government in 1614, and successor, Samuel Argall, they were put into merciless operation. The Virginia Assembly of 1624 gave a vivid account of the horrors of which they were guilty. The people "remained in great want and misery under most severe and cruel laws sent over in print, and contrary to the express letter of the King in his most gracious charter, and as mercilessly executed, often times without trial or judgment." Many fled for "relief to the savage enemy, who being taken again were put to sundry deaths as by hanging, shooting, and breaking upon the wheel." One man "for stealing of two or three pints of oatmeal had a bodkin thrust through his tongue, and was tied with a chain to a tree until he starved. . . . Many through these extremities, being weary of life, digged holes in the earth and there hid themselves till they famished."

But the dawn of a better day was at hand. In the London Company some of the leading spirits hoped to establish "a more free government in Virginia." It was only a few years later that thousands of Englishmen migrated to the wilderness of New England, in order to live there under a Puritan Church, "defended by rulers that should be of ourselves." The spirit which animated this movement might well have inspired an earlier exodus of Puritans and liberals to Virginia. When it seemed likely that King James would succeed in crushing what he considered the twin evils of Calvinism and liberalism in England, "many worthy patriots, lords, knights, gentlemen, merchants and others . . . laid hold on . . . Virginia as a providence cast before them."

Under the leadership of Sir Edwin Sandys in the Company, this group induced the King to grant a new charter in 1612, giving the Company enlarged powers. It is probable that James, in making this grant, did not suspect that they would use it to establish representative government in Virginia. In April, 1618, Lord De La Warr sailed for the colony to resume active control of affairs there, taking with him new instructions. Unfortunately De La Warr died during the voyage and we have no copy of the instructions. Though Yeardley's commission of November 18, 1618, which directed him to set up representative government in the colony, and is known as the Magna Charta of Virginia, has never been found, it no doubt corresponded closely with the constitution drawn up by the Company in July, 1621. When the Company was informed of De La Warr's death, they chose George Yeardley as his successor, and intrusted him with papers which, no doubt duplicated those given De La Warr. So when Yeardley arrived in Virginia in April, 1619, he issued a proclamation abrogating "those cruel laws" by which the people had so long been governed, and substituting "those free laws which his majesty's subjects live under in England."

This constitution set up a Council to be chosen from time to time by the Company to assist the Governor in maintaining the "people in justice and Christian conversation amongst themselves, and in strength and ability to withstand their enemies." Another body, "to be called by the Governor once yearly and no oftener but for very extraordinary and important occasions, shall consist for the present of the said Council of State, and two Burgesses out of every town, hundred, or other particular planta-

Colonial Williamsburg Photo

The Capitol, Williamsburg, Virginia
The General Assembly passed the Act for building the Capitol in 1699.

Governor's Palace, Williamsburg, Virginia
The General Assembly passed the Act for building "a house" for the Governor in 1705.

tion, to be respectively chosen by the inhabitants." This body was to be called the General Assembly. It was to "have free power to treat, consult, and conclude, as well of all emergent occasions concerning the public weal of the said colony and every part thereof, as also to make, ordain, and enact such general laws and orders . . . as shall from time to time appear necessary." To the Governor was reserved a negative voice.

The Council and the General Assembly were required "to imitate and follow the form of government, laws, customs, and manner of trial, and other ministration of justice used in the realm of England." And no law passed in the General Assembly should "continue in force" unless ratified and sealed by the Company. Then followed a provision to give the colony a degree of independence, and its government an assurance of permanence: "It being our intent to afford the like measure also unto the said colony, that after the government of the said colony shall once have been well framed . . . no orders of court afterwards shall bind the said colony, unless they be ratified in like manner in the General Assemblies."

The Assembly, the first in the New World, met on July 30, old style, in the little frame church at Jamestown. Governor Yeardley took his seat in the choir, with the members of the Council on either side. In front of them was the Speaker, and John Twine, clerk of the Assembly. Thomas Pierce, the sergeant, stood at the bar, "to be ready for any service the Assembly might command him." "But for as much as men's affairs do little prosper where God's service is neglected, all the Burgesses took their places in the choir till a prayer was said by Mr. Buck, the minister." Following this the Burgesses left the choir until each had been called by name and given the oath of supremacy. Then they resumed their seats.

It is significant that in setting up an Assembly the constitution, as worded in the document of 1621, makes no mention of a right to levy taxes. Yet in this first session it was ordered "that every man and man servant above sixteen years of age shall pay . . . one pound of the best tobacco." That they and they alone had a right to do this was taken for granted both in England and Virginia. It was only when their liberty was threatened by grants of governmental powers to royal favorites that they asked to have it incorporated in a charter, "that no imposition or tax shall be laid upon the inhabitants but by the common consent of the Governor, Council and Burgesses."

The Assembly assumed that they were the Commons of Virginia. Whatever the Commons had a right to do, they had a right to do. But they realised that their statutes would be invalid if they conflicted with the laws of England or the instructions of the London Company. Yet this left them a wide field of legislation. The first Assembly enacted laws concerning the Indians, patents for land, the Church establishment, the relation of servants and masters, the laying out of crops, morality in the colony, foreign trade, the price of tobacco, etc.

In the meanwhile James I began to show signs of hostility to the London Company. When they refused to elect as their treasurer one from a list of names he suggested, he "flung himself away in a furious passion." John Ferrar wrote: "The King, notwithstanding his royal word . . . was now determined . . . to give the death blow to this . . . Company." So Attorney-General Coventry prepared a *quo warranto* and brought the case before the King's Bench. Though the Company employed attorneys to defend their patent it was "overthrown" by a mistake in pleading.

Historians have differed as to why James destroyed the Company. Some have contended that he was chiefly actuated by political motives. They point out that he hated popular government, and that it had been whispered to him that Sir Edwin Sandys "aimed at nothing more than to make a free and popular state" in Virginia; that there were in the Company so many that were "most distasted with the proceedings of the Court and stood best affected to religion and liberty" that he began to look upon that body as a "seminary for a seditious Parliament," and that he had even gone so far as to imprison Sandys. The disasters which had plagued the Company—the frightful mortality in the colony through disease, the Indian massacre of 1622, the failure to establish industries—these writers regard as the excuse rather than the cause of the attack on the Company. This interpretation is supported by James' offer that if the Company would surrender their charter, he would grant a new one, preserving all private rights to the stockholders, but restoring the political control of the colony to the Crown.

Other historians, on the contrary, have placed the emphasis upon the economic causes. They dwell on the fact that the situation in Virginia was desperate, that the Company was divided into factions, and that it was practically bankrupt. Nothing was left to show for expenditures totaling perhaps £100,000, and the only way to wipe this charge off the books was to dissolve the Company.

It is difficult at any time to analyse men's motives; it is especially so after the lapse of three centuries. But we may at least surmise that James was influenced by both the political and economic aspects of the controversy. The commission appointed to investigate conditions in the colony may have reflected his honest opinion when they reported that the result would have been far better had his original plan been followed than by its alteration "into so popular a course."

With the dissolution of the Company the future of the colony was left in doubt. Many years afterward the Virginia Assembly stated that in October, 1623, it was promised that when the Company was dissolved, a charter would be granted to the colony wherein "the like privileges should be made to the inhabitants as were contained in the former grants." In July 1624, a special commission, headed by Henry Lord Mandeville, was appointed, with authority to make a permanent settlement of Virginia affairs. Its first action was to send a royal commission to Governor Wyatt and the Council authorizing them to exercise the same powers granted Yeardley and his successors. But they made no mention of an Assembly. Before they could conclude their work they were dissolved by the death of James I.

With the accession of Charles I the whole question of Virginia came before the Privy Council. When some of the members of the defunct Company pleaded for its re-establishment, the Council refused on the grounds that though it might be proper to commit matters of trade to a corporation, it was not safe to intrust it with the "ordering of state affairs." So they contented themselves with reappointing Sir George Yeardley Governor with the same powers recited in Wyatt's commission. Then the new King issued a proclamation declaring "that his intention was only to render this (the Virginia) government into such a right course as might best agree with the form held in the rest of his monarchy." He then outlined a plan of government, which was essentially the same as that under the charter of 1606. There was to be a Council for Virginia, resident in England, subordinate to the Privy Council and the King, and a Governor and Council in Virginia, subject to the control of the Council in England. He made no mention of an Assembly.

The people of Virginia had opposed the dissolution of the Company because they feared it might lead to the renewal of former oppression. They now pleaded for the continuing of self-government. The Governor and Council wrote the Privy Council "suggesting that the ordering of affairs in Virginia should be left to the Governor and Council, with the advice in special cases of the General Assembly." A few weeks later they wrote again asking that certain affairs "be wholly at the disposal of the Governor, Council, and General Assembly." In the meanwhile, Wyatt, and after him, Yeardley, held informal sessions of the Assembly under the title of "The Governor, Council, and Colony of Virginia assembled together." It would seem that the

"Burgesses" of these gatherings were either appointed by Wyatt or chosen in a special election, since many of them had not been members of the Assembly of 1624.

But it was not so much the pleadings of the Virginians as the accepted principle that no one, not even the King, had the right to take an Englishman's property without his own consent, which finally restored the legal status of the Assembly. Certain writers have laid stress on the need of the colony for financial support from England, but when the Virginia Company was dissolved the colony was rapidly becoming self-supporting. The discovery that Virginia tobacco could be sold at a profit in England had turned all hands to its production. Had the English government exempted the leaf from import duties, and insured a market by excluding Spanish tobacco, there would have been no need for financial assistance, either from the Company or the King.

But so far from financing the colony, both James and Charles tried to make it aid in financing the Crown. It was in March, 1628, that a certain William Capps arrived in Virginia with an offer from Charles to the planters to buy their whole annual crop. And, since he would not venture to defy acknowledged English rights by taking their property without their consent, the King gave orders for the calling of the Assembly. This, for the first time since the dissolution of the Company, gave legal status to that body. The Virginians rejected the King's offer, but they kept their Assembly. From this date the right of the people to participate in their government was unchallenged. In fact, it became habitual to insert in the instructions of a new Governor a clause directing him to hold an election of Burgesses.

Yet the colony was disturbed from time to time by attempts to revive the London Company. In 1631 a commission, nominated by the King, recommended its renewal. Charles so far yielded as to direct the Attorney-General to draw up a new charter, but in the end he withheld his consent. The people of Virginia, still remembering the "illegal proceedings and bar-

barous tortures" of former times, and anxious to place their present government upon a firmer basis, appointed George Sandys as their agent in England, apparently with instructions to apply for a charter. Instead of so doing, he petitioned the House of Commons "in the name of the adventurers and planters in Virginia" to revive the Company. When this news reached the colony the Assembly, declaring that Sandys had misunderstood his instructions, drew up a petition to the King, asking to remain under his immediate protection. Their present happiness was exemplified by their yearly Assemblies, they said, authorized in his instructions, and by legal trial by juries in criminal and civil cases. In reply Charles told them that he had not the least intention of placing any company over them.

The government thus established in Virginia remained, except for the brief interlude of the Commonwealth, to the end of the colonial period. But during the century and a half from the dissolution of the Company to the Declaration of Independence there were many important changes. There was a constant struggle for power, a struggle which at times broke out into bitter quarrels, open charges, and violent denunciations. In these conflicts the Governor represented the King, and through the King the authority of the mother country. The Council of State broadly speaking, represented the Virginia aristocracy, which in the seventeenth century was little more than a clique of closely related wealthy planters. The House of Burgesses upheld the interests of the people as a whole.

The Governor was appointed by the King. In making his selections the King seems sometimes to have followed his own inclinations, but oftener to have accepted the recommendations of the Privy Council or the Board of Trade and Plantations. Charles I chose Sir William Berkeley no doubt because he was a member of his Privy Chamber and as such had lived in his household. Culpeper owed his appointment to his loyalty to the King during his time of greatest trouble. Andros and Nicholson were professional Governors who were shifted from colony to colony.

The powers of the Governor were many and great. Back of him was the awe-inspiring person of the King. To disobey or thwart his representative might bring down his wrath upon the colony with dire consequences. When in 1684 the Burgesses positively refused to permit taxation by the Governor and Council, Effingham reported that he was sure they would never yield unless his Majesty sent a special command for them to do so.

But more tangible than the King's frown in buttressing the Governor's power was his control of the patronage. "The nomination of all places is left to the Governor," Francis Moryson wrote Secretary Arlington. "Are not all the places of profit in the hands of the Governor?" asked Benjamin Harrison. "And don't you know there is a sheriff and a clerk in every county, besides other offices of profit in the country? Is it not the wise man's phrase that a gift will blind the eyes of the wise? . . . Places are now shifted as often as the occasion requires, to put out or in, as men will or will not serve a turn."

Governor Nicholson, against whom these charges were made, defended his use of the patronage. "I always gave the offices to people that I thought more loyal and well qualified to execute them. But I confess that when my friends were so qualified I gave to them before others, which I hope is no crime in me."

Perhaps the most tempting plum which could be held out in Virginia was a seat in the Council. True, it was the King who appointed Councillors, but with rare exceptions he accepted the recommendations of the Governor. So the Burgess who had his eye on this place of honor and power, was brave indeed if he voted against any measure upon which the Governor had set his heart.

We do not know how often the Governor hinted to prominent members of the House that if they were obedient the prize might be theirs, but we have proof of one case. In 1680 Governor Culpeper reported to the Privy Council that Isaac Allerton had assured him "of his utmost services in whatsoever the King should command him by his Governor," and in return he had promised him "that he should be on the Council . . . though not to be declared till after the session of the next Assembly." This bargain was carried out, and Allerton, for betraying the interests of those who had elected him, received his seat in the Council.

Some years later, when three members of the Council were displaced because they refused to take the oath required by Parliament, Governor Nicholson selected as their successors three Burgesses who had supported the interest of the Crown. "Colonel Thomas Milner, Speaker, behaved very well too," he reported to the Lords of Trade, "but he hath not estate enough to be a Councillor. But he should have promise of some place of profit."

The Governor bound the Councillors to him by distributing among them the most lucrative offices in the colony. Of the Council of 1697 all save Colonel William Byrd II, Colonel Richard Johnston, and John Lightfoot held the offices of Collector and Naval Officer. Byrd, no doubt, was well satisfied with his job as Auditor, Johnston had to be content with his place as escheator, and Lightfoot had just joined the Council. If a Councillor turned against the Governor, or opposed important measures he was trying to push through the Assembly, he ran the risk of being put out of his various jobs or even being suspended from the Council. In 1686 Governor Effingham wrote: "I have suspended Colonel Philip Ludwell from the Council, as having great reason to believe him to be an instrument in abetting and fomenting disputes in the Assembly." In the sessions of the Council he had urged against the King's interest, instead of advocating it "as he ought." Effingham had a few months previously given him a collector's place, "in hopes to have gained him by it," so he now suspended him from that also.

This case throws light on the influence of the Governor over officials appointed by the King himself. The Surveyor-General of the colony at the time, Alexander Culpeper, had appointed Ludwell his deputy, with authority to name the surveyors. Effingham, during a meeting of the Council, ordered Ludwell to put Major Arthur Allen "out of his surveyor's place," as not thinking it fit that those who are peevishly opposite to his Majesty's interest should have any advantage by his favor. And he was highly displeased when Ludwell "immediately gave it to one Major Swan, one altogether as troublesome as the other."

The Governor won the support of scores of prominent men by handing out military offices with a lavish hand. Of the thirty members of the House of Burgesses of 1660, six were colonels of militia, two lieutenant-colonels, one a major, and fourteen were captains. The county courts also took on a military aspect. Among the York justices in the years from 1658 to 1676 were a colonel, a lieutenant-colonel, several majors, and many captains. There seem to have been no salaries attached to these offices except in times of war, but they carried great prestige. The man who was bold enough to speak disrespectfully to a colonel or a major was lucky if he escaped a fine or imprisonment.

The Governors were empowered by their instructions to appoint "judges, justices of the peace, sheriffs, and other officers." This gave them a commanding hand in local government. In their selections the Governor was often influenced by the court itself, and he always gave consideration to their recommendations. But he was sure to reject anyone, however influential in his county, who had shown an independent spirit in opposing his policies or the King's orders. From an early date it was customary for the sheriff of a county to be a member of the court, and by an act of Assembly in 1661 this was made compulsory. The sheriff's office entailed the onerous duty of collecting the poll tax, but it carried a handsome income and was invested with great dignity.

The Governor frequently turned to the Council for advice in appointing local officials. It was impossible for him to know every eligible candidate, especially in distant counties; if he were a new arrival he would have an especially limited acquaintance with even the most prominent planters. So, if it were necessary to appoint a justice or a sheriff in a certain county, he would ask the Councillor who resided there or nearby to make recommendations. Eventually the Council came to regard this as a right, and were bitterly resentful if a Governor ignored them in making appointments. One of the complaints against Francis Nicholson was that he had nominated sheriffs "without the advice of the Council contrary to all former practices," and that in like manner he had put in and turned out "all colonels, lieutenant-colonels, majors, captains, and other officers of the militia."

The Governor had the right to call, to prorogue, and to dissolve the Assembly. If he secured a House of Burgesses to his liking, he might continue it indefinitely by a series of prorogations. Sir William Berkeley kept the famous Long Assembly for at least fourteen years. But on the arrival of a new Governor, or the accession of a King, the Assembly was automatically dissolved.

The Governor had an absolute veto over legislation. But he often found it unnecessary to make use of this power, since if he disapproved of a bill, he could oppose it when it came up to the Council, and, except in the rare cases when the members were hostile to him, persuade that body to kill it. Or, if he was opposed to a bill which was so universally desired that to veto it would cause resentment in both Houses of the Assembly, he might sign it, trusting to the King to disallow it.

The Governor exercised a powerful influence in the administration of justice. He presided over the General Court, and could, and at times did, browbeat both witnesses and judges, in order to secure a verdict of his liking. Philip Ludwell said that the influence of the Governor "both on judges and witnesses" was very great, "particularly by the multitude of places and other favors he has to promise in case they favor him in the trial, and partly by the certain ruin they must expect if they do otherwise." In the case of Swan versus Wilson Governor Nicholson so greatly abused Swan's attorney "that everybody cried out shame." Since the Governor appointed the justices of the peace who constituted the county courts, his influence over local justice was equally great.

The Governor was also the legal head of the established Church. He had the right to induct ministers after they had been presented by the vestries. He also claimed the right of collation to vacant parishes, but since this was bitterly opposed by the vestries, he seldom tried to exercise it. Late in the seventeenth century the Bishop of London, who acted as diocesan for the Anglican Church in the colonies, appointed a Commissary to represent him in Virginia. This led to divided authority in ecclesiastical affairs, and at times to bitter disputes between the Commissary and the Governor.

If we turn now to the Council of State, intended originally to serve only as an advisory body for the Governor, we find that in time they assumed also other functions. Hartwell, Blair, and Chilton, in their *The Present State of Virginia*, thus summarize their duties and privileges: "They are the Council of State under the Governor, who always presides; and in the vacancy of a Governor and Lieutenant-Governor, the eldest of the Council is President. They are the Upper House of Assembly, answering to the House of Peers in England. They are by custom, but without commission, the supreme judges (together with the Governor who presides) in all causes, viz. in chancery, King's Bench, common pleas, exchequer, admiralty, and spirituality, and there lies no appeal from them but to the King in Council . . . They are colonels and commanders-in-chief of the several counties, in the nature of the Lords Lieutenants in England.

They are naval officers. . . . They are collectors. . . . They are the farmers of the King's quit rents. . . . Out of them are chosen the Secretary, Auditor, and escheators."

The members were invariably picked from the wealthiest and most influential men in the colony. They could boast of their many acres, of their indentured workers and slaves, of their cattle and sheep, of their silver, of their libraries. In their own counties they played the part of petty lords. Philip Alexander Bruce says: "The social gulf lying between powerful and wealthy citizens like the older William Byrd, Richard Lee, or Nicholas Spencer and the obscure proprietor owning an adjacent estate of a few hundred acres, was as great as that dividing the English nobleman from a neighbor who occupied the same position in life as the Virginia yeoman."

As the Privy Council of the colony the Council could and did exert great influence over the Governor. In certain matters he was obliged by his instructions to consult them; in others, especially in perplexing situations, he was glad to have their advice. Berkeley said that he never resisted the opinion of his Council. This may have been an exaggeration, but we know that he turned to them for counsel in the moment of peril when his government was threatened by Bacon and his army. In fact, no Governor was so certain of his own opinion that he habitually scorned advice. If an Indian war threatened, if the low price of tobacco caused a plant-cutting riot, if the Burgesses had openly defied the King's orders, if a fleet of Dutch warships had invaded Chesapeake Bay, the Governor was certain to consult his legally constituted advisors.

Councillors were always members of the Assembly. Originally they sat with the Burgesses, and did not constitute a separate House. In one respect this limited their power, since they never exceeded twelve in number and so could always be outvoted. In another respect it actually increased their influence, for it gave them the opportunity to enter into debates with the Burgesses and to sit on important committees. Then, in 1680, came an important change. The historian Beverley says that "Lord Culpeper, taking advantage of some disputes among them, procured the Council to sit apart from the Assembly, so that they became two distinct Houses, in imitation of the two Houses of Parliament."

Although this change gave the Council the right to block legislation, it had for them the disadvantage of placing them in legislative matters, as they already were in administrative and judicial concerns, directly under the influence of the Governor. The Governor presided over their meetings, and it was seldom indeed that they voted contrary to his wishes. If they ever became refractory, he had only to remind them that they held their positions by appointment of the King. In voting for measures which they knew to be inconsistent with the interests of the colony, they salved their consciences with the thought that they could safely leave it to the Burgesses to defeat them. They might even vote one way in Council, and privately urge members of the House to vote the other way. This explains why the Governor was apt to be suspicious if he saw a Councillor hobnobbing with the Burgesses.

The members of the Council were extremely jealous of their judicial power. Perhaps this was because it rested upon custom alone and had no legal sanction. Early in the eighteenth century, when Governor Spotswood tried to weaken it by holding a court of oyer and terminer with others than Councillors on the bench, they resisted vigorously and successfully. But in the General Court, as in the upper House of Assembly, the Governor presided and his views often dominated the decisions. After 1680 no appeals were permitted from this court except to the King and Privy Council, and then only in causes involving £300 sterling or more. As a result appeals were rare, for the cost of taking witnesses across the Atlantic and other necessary charges were prohibitive. In 1691 the Council and the Burgesses instructed their agent in England to seek an order forbidding appeals to the King and Privy Council because of "the difficulty, charge, and impossibility of either prosecuting or defending matters at such a distance."

The Council reached the height of its power in the last decade of the seventeenth century and the first two decades of the eighteenth century. Colonel Robert Quarry, who for a brief time sat with them and was well acquainted with their proceedings, said that they "had vanity enough to think themselves almost upon equal terms with the House of Lords." Nicholson stated that it was easy to see that they wanted to have all the power in their own hands, and that if everything they wanted were granted them, "his Majesty would have but a skeleton of a government left." They were angry with him he added, "because he would not be governed by them, and turn secretaries, auditors, collectors, naval officers, and others out of their places, and put them and their friends in. . . . I think the question may be put to them as the wise King Solomon did to his mother, 'Why don't they ask the Kingdom?'"

What so disturbed Nicholson was the knowledge that several members of the Council had preferred charges of misgovernment against him before the Committee of Trade and Plantations. He knew that a group, headed by Commissary Blair, had been responsible for the removal of Andros, and he feared that it might be his turn next. "Mr. Blair and his little faction now set up to have the power and interest of turning out and putting in Governors, and affect the title that the great Earl of Warwick had," he wrote. It was not long after he had penned this that he was notified that he had been displaced.

The champions of the people were the Burgesses. The small planter, the tradesman, the freedman looked to them for protection against any infringement of their liberties or disregard of their interests by King, Governor, or Council. Throughout the entire colonial period, with rare exceptions when they were either bribed or intimidated, they were faithful to their trust. Again and again the Governors reported that they were stubborn or "undutiful" in opposing the King's interest, or in infringing upon his prerogative. The nadir of the Burgesses was during the Restoration Period, when the Long Assembly seems to have been little more than a rubber stamp for Governor Berkeley, and the Second Stuart Despotism, when its privileges and powers were assailed by Charles II and James II. Their zenith came in the second and third quarter of the eighteenth century, when they became the real rulers of Virginia.

We do not know who had the right to vote for the Burgesses in the first Assembly. The Constitution of 1621 specified that the Burgesses be chosen by the "inhabitants". It would seem probable, then, that prior to 1670, with the exception of one year, every freeman had the right to vote. In 1663, Governor Berkeley proposed that taxation be imposed, not by poll, but upon landowners only, in proportion to their acreage. The Burgesses objected that since the right to vote belonged only to taxpayers, this would disfranchise "the other freemen, who are more in numbers . . . and we are so well acquainted with the temper of the people that we have reason to believe they had rather pay their tax than lose their privilege."

But seven years later, no doubt under the urging of Berkeley, they reversed their position, and passed a law limiting the suffrage to freeholders and housekeepers. In defense of their action they argued that indentured workers "having served their time are freemen of this country, who, having little interest in the country, do oftener make tumults at the elections" than show any discretion in their votes. They also pointed out that the franchise in England was limited to persons having property enough "to tie them to the endeavor of the public good."

It is significant that it was the Long Assembly which made this change. Whereas in 1663 it had the courage to oppose the Governor, by 1670 it had fallen so much under his influence that they were obedient to his will. At the time Berkeley was alarmed at the large number of poor men who were coming to the colony, and complained that Virginia was "but a sink to drain England" of its rabble. And he was fearful that the poverty, discontent, and lawlessness of the lower class might lead to a rebellion. Six years later, when a rebellion actually occurred, he tried to appease the people by dissolving the Long Assembly and calling for an election, in which "every free born man's vote" was to be counted. And the new Assembly, under the pressure of Bacon's army, confirmed this ruling by passing a law granting the suffrage to all freemen.

But with the repeal of Bacon's Laws the act of 1670 went into effect again. In 1679, when Culpeper was Governor, he was instructed to make a further restriction, by depriving mere housekeepers of the right to vote, and limiting it to freeholders. "This punctually performed," he reported to the Lords of Trade and Plantations. Since Effingham and Andros received similar instructions it would seem that freeholders alone voted during the remainder of the century.

The presiding officer of the House of Burgesses was the Speaker, elected by a majority vote of the members. It was a position of great honor and influence, eagerly sought after. In 1699, when five men were nominated, the votes were divided 20 to 20 for two of them and remained so through numerous ballots. It was only with the arrival of lagging Burgesses that the tie was broken and Mr. Robert Carter elected. In his address of acceptance Carter said: "The House of Burgesses consisting of the better sort of gentlemen from all parts of the country, to be in this fashion the object of their choice I take to be no small reputation to me." He was then, according to custom, presented to the Governor, who gave his approval of his choice. The Speaker moved his Excellency "for the continuance of the ancient privileges of the House of free access to his Excellency's person . . . and that they might have freedom of speech and debate in the House, and that themselves and servants might be free from arrest." To these things the Governor gave a ready assent, and the Speaker withdrew.

As the power of the House increased with time, so did that of the Speaker. By the mid-eighteenth century he rivalled the Governor as the most influential man in the colony.

The clerk of the House of Burgesses kept the journal of its proceedings, and, after 1680, sent a copy to the Lords of Trade and Plantations. But though the records were open to inspection, they were closely guarded. In 1677, the King's Commissioners in their investigation of the causes of Bacon's Rebellion, came to Major Robert Beverley, the clerk, and demanded "all the original journals, orders, acts," etc. then in his custody. When he refused, they took them by violence. The Burgesses protested to Colonel Jeffreys, who was head of the commission, that this was a great violation of their privileges. They were sure the King would not have authorized such a thing, since none of his predecessors had done so. They asked him "please to give the House such satisfaction that they may be assured no such violation of their privileges shall be offered for the future." Charles II was greatly angered that they should thus call in question his authority, and asked the Lords of Trade what should be done to bring the Burgesses to a sense of their "duty and submission."

Eight years later Beverley again brought down the royal anger on the House. A certain bill which came up to the Council was assented to by them and the Governor, but with an amendment attached. This Beverley tore off, and after the Burgesses had assented, returned the bill without it. Neither the Governor nor the Council noticed the omission, and thinking the amendment had been accepted, signed the bill. But when the engrossed copy came before the Governor he discovered the omission and refused to affix his name. This so angered the Burgesses that they refused to levy the tax for defraying the public charges.

For this the King not only rebuked them, but struck a blow

at their privileges by depriving them of the right to elect their clerk. In 1686, Secretary Nicholas Spencer wrote the Lords of Trade and Plantations that the clerk of the House ought to be appointed by the Governor, and paid out of the royal revenue. "This will take off his dependency on his great masters, the House of Burgesses, and leave no room for designed omissions." The King approved the suggestion, and directed Effingham to carry it out. So, in April, 1688, when the Governor named Captain Francis Page clerk, the House was forced to yield. And though at the first session of the Assembly after the Glorious Revolution, they quietly resumed the right to choose their clerk, their success was short-lived. In 1692 Andros insisted on appointing the clerk, and succeeding Governors followed his example.

The business of the House was largely transacted through committees, each with its own chairman and clerk. The most important was the Committee on Propositions and Grievances. Before it came all manner of complaints, some from individual counties, some from certain groups, some from one or more persons. Now it is a complaint by the Quakers of Henrico of the severity of the law against them for not bearing arms and not attending musters; now it is a request from York County that justices of the peace be forbidden to take fees; now the people of Elizabeth City County ask that tavern keepers be fined for selling liquor to sailors after eight o'clock at night; now certain planters ask to have the size of tobacco hogsheads changed; now others want a more vigorous enforcement of the law against meetings of slaves.

The House jealously guarded its control over elections, and always named some of the most prominent members to the Committee of Elections and Privileges. This committee went over the writs of return, and if any irregularity was detected, reported it to the House. In the session of 1692 the sheriffs of Norfolk and Northumberland Counties were summoned before the Burgesses and ordered to change their returns. When two writs for the same seat came in from Elizabeth City County, one for Mr. Willis Willson and the other for Mr. William Armistead, both men were called in to argue their cases. But when it was brought out that Willson was "under age," his claim was disallowed, and Armistead seated.

A heavy responsibility rested on the Committee for Proportioning the Levy, for they had to consider the innumerable claims for services rendered. If they failed to satisfy all claimants they were criticised; when all payments had been made they were criticised because the total was so large. The Committee on Private Causes, in the long period before the Assembly was deprived of its judicial powers, was in reality the supreme court of appeals, for its recommendations were usually accepted without question.

When a committee was appointed to handle some especially important matter it was customary to ask the Council to appoint two or more of its members to sit with them. But on one occasion, at least, some of the Burgesses protested against this practice. In the Assembly of June, 1676, it was proposed that the Governor be requested to assign two of his Council to sit with the Committee on Indian Affairs, "as had been usual." This produced an uproar, "one party urging hard that it was customary," others contending that if they had bad customs they had come there to mend them. In the end the matter was "huddled off without coming to vote, and so the committee must submit to be overawed, and have every carped at expression carried straight to the Governor."

The House of Burgesses attached great importance to its dignity, and was quick to punish any reflection on any individual member. In 1693 a certain Thomas Rooke, in an altercation with Mathew Kemp, a Burgess from Middlesex, "abused and struck him," using "gross words and speeches not fit to be repeated." He also reflected against the honor of the House in general. He was arrested and forced on his bended knees to beg the

House to accept his hearty contrition, and to promise that for the future he would behave himself with all due reverence towards the representatives "of this their Majesties' most ancient colony."

The Burgesses stoutly maintained that the Assembly alone had a right to tax the people. They conceded that the English Parliament might tax them indirectly through their power to regulate the trade of the empire, but at the least suggestion that they consent to internal taxes by any other body than themselves, they were up in arms. It is true that in 1661 they gave permission to Governor Berkeley and the Council to lay taxes for three years not to exceed twenty pounds of tobacco, but five years later, when Berkeley requested that two or more Councillors be permitted to sit with the House in laying the levy, he met with a decided rebuff. The Burgesses answered that it was their privilege to lay the levy, but they admitted that after they had done so, it must be presented to the Council for their approval or dissent. Berkeley took this in good part, and thought that it should be "a rule to walk by for the future."

In 1679, when Culpeper was leaving for Virginia, he was instructed to ask the Assembly to grant permission to the Governor and Council to levy taxes not exceeding twenty pounds of tobacco per poll. In urging compliance Culpeper pointed out that this would lessen the burden of taxation, since at times the cost of holding an Assembly was twice as much "as would have satisfied all public dues." But the Burgesses flatly refused. Governor Effingham, some years later, also was rebuffed when he made the same request.

But in 1680 the Assembly made a concession which was unique in the American colonies, and threatened the very foundations of liberty. In 1661 an act had been passed laying a duty of two shillings a hogshead on tobacco exported from the colony. It was stated in the act that the collectors were to dispose of this revenue only "by order of the Grand Assembly." When Culpeper came to the colony in 1680 he brought with him a bill drawn up by the English Attorney-General, assented to by the King, and passed under the Great Seal of England, to secure a permanent revenue for the King, in order to free him as far as possible from the power of the Assembly. The bill was similar to the act of 1661, but with the vital difference that the money was to be granted "to the King's most excellent Majesty, his heirs and successors forever, to and for the better support of the government."

When Culpeper demanded that they pass this measure the Burgesses were dismayed. Why this was asking them to surrender their most precious gem. "The House do most humbly desire to be excused if they do not give their approbation of his Majesty's Bill," they told Culpeper. So determined were they, that when the matter was brought before them again, they refused even to consider it.

But the Governor used every weapon at his disposal to bring them into line. We have his own word that he won over one member with the offer of a seat in the Council, and it is probable that he handed out fat jobs with a lavish hand. Nor did he hesitate to use threats. The quit rents had not been duly collected for many years, so that the accumulated arrears now amounted to a great sum. Should the King insist that this be paid, it would bring ruin to perhaps a majority of the Burgesses. Culpeper reminded them of this, pointing out that they were not in a position to defy him. "Consider the affairs of the quit rents," he said, "consider the King's favor in everything you may ask." Then he hinted that if they refused to grant this revenue, the King might take it without their consent. His Majesty considered it his own, he said, and should the act fail would not only claim it, but perhaps increase the duty. This was a strange threat, indeed, for the King had no right to change the provisions of the existing law by diverting the revenue to himself. If the Assembly continued to balk at the new law the only legal way he could have got it was by an act of Parliament, and that would have been taxation without representation. Nonetheless, the Burgesses finally yielded, and, with minor amendments, passed the bill.

Thus the cause of self-government in colonial Virginia suffered its greatest reverse. No longer could the Assembly force the Governor to sign their bills by refusing to vote his salary. No longer did they hold a sword over the heads of the Councillors. It is true that they still retained in part their grip upon the purse, since the export duty together with the quit rents seldom met even the ordinary needs of the government, and were entirely inadequate in times of emergency. It is this which explains why such notable gains for liberty were made during the colonial wars. Yet from the passage of this bill until the Declaration of Independence the Virginia Assembly had to fight the royal prerogative with one hand tied behind its back.

The most important source of revenue was the poll tax, imposed on all tithables. The definition of a tithable changed from time to time throughout the century, but usually it meant all white males over sixteen years of age, all white women over sixteen who tilled the ground, and all slaves old enough to work. In 1704 there were 19,715 tithables in Virginia exclusive of the Northern Neck. The poll tax was used to produce revenue not only for the general government, but for the counties and the parishes.

The poor planters denounced this tax as unfair. The rich man's income might be twenty times that of his neighbor, but his taxes perhaps only five times as great. Why did the rich not have to pay taxes on their land holdings, on their herds of cattle and sheep, and on their houses and silverware? In 1663 the Governor and Council admitted that the poll tax was unjust in a resolution declaring "the most equal way of paying taxes is by laying a levy upon land and not upon heads." But, strangely enough, the Burgesses failed to take advantage of this opportunity, and the levy by poll remained. The people, however, continued to complain. Just prior to Bacon's Rebellion, the Virginia agents in England said their chief grievance was "the great and unequal taxes by poll, when a land tax were, as they say, more easy and equal."

Although the small planter complained so bitterly when the sheriff took part of his little crop of tobacco, the tax was usually not excessive according to modern standards. The Virginia agents said in 1676 that taxes in Virginia were less than in any other government in America. In 1667 Thomas Ludwell stated that 1,200 pounds was the average crop of tobacco for one man. Now the poll tax for York County in 1666 was 68½ pounds a tithable. If we add 30 pounds for parish dues, the total comes to about nine per cent, which was probably not far from the average throughout the colony. But for the poor man, who had been forced to take up infertile land on the frontier because of the large holding of the influential group, the crop would be smaller and the percentage paid in taxes proportionately heavier.

A large degree of relief came in the closing decades of the century. The duty of two shillings per hogshead yielded more and more as the exports of tobacco doubled and tripled. William Fitzhugh estimated the revenue from this source at £4,000 in 1687. Since the Governor was now paid out of this fund, and not as formerly from the levy by poll, one of the heaviest drains on the latter came to an end. Just how heavy this drain had been is shown by the fact that York County alone paid the Governor 20,000 pounds of tobacco for the year 1660, 34,115 for 1661, and 13,199 for 1665.

It was at the suggestion of the Lords of Trade that the Assembly, in 1684, placed a duty upon the importation of wines, brandy, and other liquors. From this source came a revenue of about £600, equivalent at the time to 144,000 pounds of tobacco. Another duty imposed on the importation of servants and slaves, still further reduced the poll tax. Just how great was the relief from these various sources is shown by the fact that the planter in Lancaster, who had paid on an average 118 pounds annually in the years from 1674 to 1683, paid only 39 pounds in the period from 1687 to 1699. The Lower Norfolk planter must have rejoiced that his annual tax dropped from 64 pounds in the period from 1666 to 1683, to twenty-six pounds in the years from 1685 to 1691.

The quit rent fund, though belonging to the Crown, was drawn on during certain emergencies which otherwise would have made it necessary to increase the poll tax. In theory all the land in the colony belonged to the King, so that in granting it out, he had the right to require a perpetual rental. In Virginia this rental was one shilling annually for every fifty acres, payable in tobacco at one penny per pound. The cost of collecting the quit rents was great; it was found impossible to make large landowners pay in full; there were habitual frauds in disposing of the tobacco, and at times hundreds of planters were in arrears in their payments. Yet the revenue was of considerable importance. Beverley states that it was "upwards of 1200 pounds a year" sterling. The amount collected in 1705 was £1,841.1.6¾.

This fund was to be drawn upon in any "sudden and dangerous emergency," such as war or rebellion. But it was used, also, for the support of the government, for the building of forts, paying salaries, etc. When Governor Hunter was captured by the French on his way to Virginia, he was granted £1,418.5 out of the quit rents, "as compensation for the loss of his equipage." In 1693 King William and Queen Mary gave an order for £1,985.14.10 from the quit rents to Commissary Blair for the new college which bore their name. The money was paid despite the opposition of Attorney-General Seymour, who said it could be put to better uses. When Commissary Blair explained that the chief purpose of the college was to train young men for the ministry, and reminded him that the people of Virginia had souls to be saved as well as the people of England, he snapped: "Damn your souls! Make tobacco."

Throughout most of the seventeenth century the Assembly was the highest tribunal of the colony. When a case was appealed from the General Court to the Assembly it was turned over to a joint committee of the two Houses, whose decisions were usually accepted without question. Thus the Assembly was a refuge for those who thought themselves wronged by the decisions of the lower courts.

In 1682 Governor Culpeper received instructions not to "allow of any appeals whatsover to be made from the Governor and Council to the Assembly." But Culpeper, who was interested only in getting money out of the Burgesses, hesitated to ask them to repeal the laws covering appeals, "well knowing how infinitely it would trouble them." On the other hand, Effingham had no such scruples, and he had no sooner taken office in 1684 than he laid the King's command before them. Deeply troubled, the House requested Governor and Council to join them in an address to the King, asking him not to forbid a practice so long enjoyed. But Effingham refused to do so, and henceforth justice in the colony was left entirely in the hands of the Governor and the Council, and the Governor's appointees in the county courts.

In a long letter to Secretary Arlington in 1666, Thomas Ludwell wrote: "This colony is divided at present into nineteen counties ... each left to the care and charge of eight or ten justices of the peace ... by commission from the Governor made and constituted a court of judicature." They were empowered to try all causes "except as question life, or member." Individual justices tried "any cause to the value of twenty shillings or two hundred pounds of tobacco." Before the county courts came a wide variety of cases. Now we find the justices imposing a fine for theft, now they probate a will, now they attach an estate for the payment of a debt, now a runaway slave is placed in the stocks, now a man is forced to pay heavy damages for getting a female servant with child.

The legislative and administrative duties of the court were of minor importance. They might give orders for the construction of a bridge over a creek, or the operation of a ferry over one of the great rivers, or for the erection of a courthouse. They often granted land within their counties as a reward for the importation of settlers. On one occasion York County sent men to Accomac to assist in a war with the Indians there. One court ordered the payment to Governor Berkeley of one bushel of corn for every tithable for his private use.

On the bench sat usually some of the leading men of the county. They had large estates, were often officers in the militia, from their number it was customary to choose the representatives of the county in the House of Burgesses. Though the office carried no salary, it gave the incumbent great prestige, and the dignity of the court was guarded jealously. In 1685 a certain Stephen Chilton, for insulting one of the justices of the Lancaster court, was placed in the stocks. Four years later Charles Holden, attorney for the King, lost his temper in the Northampton court and let loose a volley of oaths. He was fortunate to get off with a fine of fifty pounds of tobacco.

Although the people had no voice in choosing the justices, the justices had the power to tax them. This was a clear violation of the principle that no man's money should be taken without his own consent, and was a source of suspicion and discontent. After Bacon's Rebellion the people of Charles City County complained that the justices "have illegally . . . taken upon them without our consent from time to time to impose, raise, assess, and levy what taxes, levies, and impositions upon us . . . they liked, great part of which they have converted to their own use." The reform Assembly of 1676 had sought to remedy this situation by giving all freemen the right to vote for representatives equal in numbers with the justices to sit and vote with them in laying the county levy. The same representatives were to have an equal voice also in "making wholesome bylaws." But this attempt to make local government more democratic failed with the voiding of Bacon's Laws.

The county levy was often heavier than the public levy. In the period from 1685 to 1699 the public levy for Middlesex averaged 20,165 pounds a year, the county levy 26,759. The Essex public levy from 1692 to 1699 totaled 49,568, the county levy 224,632. The chief item of expense in the local budget was the salary and expenses of the county's representatives in the House of Burgesses.

Every county had one or more parishes, each under the direction of a vestry. To this body was entrusted the nomination of the minister, the payment of his salary, the erection of the church and one or more chapels, ecclesiastical discipline, the providing for the aged and poor, taking care of orphaned children, and laying the parish levy. The minister charged with "excess in drinking, or riot, or spending his time idly by day or night, playing at dice, cards, or any other unlawful game" would have to explain his conduct to his outraged vestry. If they preferred charges against him before the Governor and Council, he would be fortunate if he escaped suspension. Ecclesiastical discipline extended, not only to the clergy but to laymen. In 1639 Robert Sweet, who ranked as a gentleman, was ordered to appear in church in a white sheet, for improper relations with a servant girl. In Northampton, in 1648, the wife of a prominent citizen was accused before the vestry of infidelity to her husband, found guilty, and presented by the minister and churchwardens to the county court for punishment.

The power of the vestry to tax the parishioners, made it a matter of great importance that they should be elected by the people. The parish levy was always heavy, and in some instances exceeded that of either the public or county levy. In 1645 the Assembly passed an act providing "that the election of every vestry be in the power of the major part of the parishioners, who being warned, shall appear to make choice of such men as by plurality of voices shall be thought fit." This democratic method seems to have persisted until sometime during Berkeley's second administration. Then, at least some of the vestries began themselves to fill vacancies in their ranks, and thus to become self-perpetuating bodies.

The long continuance of vestries was presented as a grievance to the King's commissioners after Bacon's Rebellion. The people of Surry complained that they had "not had liberty to choose vestrymen," and asked that "the whole parish may have a free election." Northampton asked "that we may have liberty granted to choose a new vestry, and that every three years a vestry may be chosen." Isle of Wight made the same request. In response to like appeals, the Assembly of June, 1676, passed an act giving the freemen of every parish the right to elect vestrymen whenever they wished by a majority vote.

After this law was voided, there seem to have been elections only when a new parish was established. Beverley says that "the vestries were at first chosen by the vote of the parishoners, but upon the death of one, have been continued by the survivors' electing another in his place." Hartwell, Blair, and Chilton, in their *The Present State of Virginia*, make a similar statement. The vestry was chosen at first by all the masters of families, they say, but they had "power to continue themselves, for as one dies or removes out of the parish, the remaining vestrymen choose another in his room." We may follow this process in the *Vestry Book of St. Paul's Parish,* of Hanover County. The vestry was elected by the freeholders and housekeepers in 1704, but after that it became a self-perpetuating body. When Mr. David Crawford died the vestry chose Mr. William England in his place, when Mr. England died they chose Mr. William Meriwether, when Mr. Robert Anderson died they elected Mr. Joseph Baughon. And so it continued until the vestry was dissolved by the Assembly during the Revolution, and a new one elected by the people.

The vestries were the dominant power in the established church. The Bishop of London, 1675, acted as diocesan of all the colonies, but in practice he had little authority. In 1689 he appointed the Reverend James Blair as his Commissary, with power to hold convocations, make visitations, and supervise the conduct of the clergy. Since the Governor claimed by his commission the right to induct and collate ministers, the Church had two heads, each with very limited authority. Consequently the vestries did pretty much what they pleased.

The basis of their power was their control of the parish purse. In England wealthy patrons, who had perhaps endowed a parish, presented the minister to the bishop for induction. But in Virginia the vestry, who had built the church and who paid the minister his salary, claimed the right to select him. In a few cases they did present clergymen for induction, but most of the clergy officiated only as their salaried employees.

Governor Nicholson made a determined effort to force the vestries to present their ministers, and even secured an opinion from Attorney-General Edward Northey, that in cases where they refused to do so he had the right to collate. But the vestries defied both Nicholson and Northey, and, one after the other, refused to obey. In the end the Governor had to submit, for had he forced his nominee on a parish, the vestry would have withheld his salary and starved him out.

Turning now to administrative positions other than that of Governor, we find that the President of the Council, Secretary of State, Attorney-General, Auditor, and Treasurer, were the most important. It was the custom for the Councillor having had the longest term of service to become President when the office of the Governor became temporarily vacant, until a new Governor arrived. For this reason one's rank in the Council was jealously guarded. The President exercised all the powers of the Governor, and as recompense for his services received £500 a year. Among the early Presidents were Captain Nathaniel Powell, Captain Francis West, Dr. John Pott, and Captain John West. In 1644, when Sir William Berkeley went to England, Richard Kemp became President. The practice of making the senior Councillor President had the disadvantage of entrusting vitally important duties to a man perhaps too old to carry them out properly. When Nathaniel Bacon Senior became President he was 68 years old, President Robert Carter was 69.

The Secretary of State was appointed by the King, usually upon the recommendation of the Governor. The office was held by a succession of prominent men—William Claiborne, Richard Kemp, Richard Lee, Thomas Ludwell, Philip Ludwell, Daniel Parke. It became customary for the Secretary to leave the work to clerks, who only too often were incompetent or neglectful. Thomas Ludwell was absent for many months when he was agent for the colony in England.

If we may believe Benjamin Harrison, the office was a hodgepodge of all kinds of business. "In it are kept the records of all proceedings in the General Court." Piled up together were judgments in capital, criminal, and civil causes. "Ecclesiastical cases are here kept, or pretended to be kept," here were registries of births, burials, marriages, and inductions of ministers. Here were returned writs of election of Burgesses, surveys of land, inquisitions of escheat, coroners' inquests, fines and forfeitures, certificates for rights to land, etc. "Many people have suffered by the ill management of that office, and nothing hath been more common of late years than to have people complain that they could not find the records of their patents or other deeds for lands. If any particular man had taken the trouble to look narrowly into the office he would quickly have found faults enough."

Like the Secretary of State, the Auditor received his commission from the King, usually upon the nomination of the Governor. It was he who audited the quit rents, the returns from the export duty of two shillings per hogshead, and the income from fines and forfeitures, escheats, etc. His was a fat job, for he received 7½ per cent of all the money collected. Among the Auditors were Thomas Stegg, Edward Digges, Nathaniel Bacon, Senior and William Byrd II.

The Treasurer's duty was to receive from the collectors the funds from the various levies, and make up the accounts. He received six per cent of the money passing through his hands. The Treasurer seems to have been appointed by the King until 1681, when the Burgesses won a vital victory by naming a Treasurer of their own to receive all taxes voted by the Assembly.

Among the other officers were the escheators, collectors, naval officers, surveyors, county clerks, and sheriffs. Naval officers received large fees from vessels entering or clearing from the colony, plus 10 per cent of the income from the export duty on tobacco. The collectors had a salary from the English treasury, in addition to 20 per cent of the duties paid them, and fees for entering and clearing. The clerks of county courts were appointed by the Secretary of State. They were paid stated fees for their services, which in populous counties brought in ample incomes. The sheriff also received large fees. But the larger part of the sheriff's income came from the 10 per cent paid him out of the poll tax in his county.

In any study of government in the seventeenth century it must be remembered that changes were constantly being made. Some of these affected the fundamental constitution, such as the restricting of the franchise, or the withdrawal of the right of the Assembly to act as a court of appeals, or the electing of a Treasurer by the Assembly, or the making the vestries self-perpetuating. Even more important were the more subtle changes which showed themselves in the spirit of the times. The House of Burgesses which submitted tamely to the "French despotism" of Sir William Berkeley was a very different body from the House which fought Governor Nicholson so bitterly despite his shameful use of the patronage. The Council which ate out of Berkeley's hand contrasted with the body which was instrumental in ousting Andros, Nicholson, and Spotswood.

To understand these changes it is necessary to trace briefly some of the more important political developments. As we have seen, the people of Virginia were fortunate in establishing representative government during the first Stuart Despotism, but it was not without effort that they were able to maintain it. Several of their early Governors respected the people's rights and defended their liberties. But in 1630 Charles I sent them a Governor more in sympathy with his own views, and, it would seem, of a despotic disposition. Sir John Harvey proved to be one of the worst colonial Governors. He had hardly set foot on Virginia soil, when he tried to impress the people with his power by ruining Dr. Pott, who as President of the Council, had preceded him in the government. Accusing him of "pardoning wilful murder, marking other men's cattle for his own and killing up their hogs," he suspended him from the Council, brought him to trial, and confiscated his estate. "It will be a means to bring the people to . . . hold a better respect to the Governor," he said.

If we may believe the historian Charles Campbell, Harvey was a tyrant. "He was extortionate, proud, unjust, and arbitrary. He issued proclamations in derogation of the legislative powers of the Assembly; assessed, levied, held, and disbursed the colonial revenues without check or responsibility; transplanted into Virginia exotic statutes; multiplied penalties and exactions; appropriated fines for his own use." Sir John Wolstenholm, who kept in close touch with the colony, stated that Harvey's misconduct was notorious at Court and in London.

An especial bit of arbitrariness aroused the anger of the Council. When a certain Captain Young, who came to Virginia upon a commission from the King, seized a skilled servant of one of the planters to construct two shallops, Harvey gave his assent.

It was done, he said, "to prosecute with speed the King's service." The Council protested that this action violated an act of Assembly, and when they received no satisfaction, "departed from the Governor in a very irreverent manner." Perhaps it was just as well that they left, for on another occasion Harvey struck one of them with a cudgel and knocked out some of his teeth. Another Councillor complained that the Governor had usurped the powers of the courts, "whereby justice was now done but so far as suited his will, to the great loss of many men's estates and a general fear in all."

The crisis came in 1635. When Harvey refused to forward to the King a paper drawn up by the Assembly in answer to his proposal to buy all the tobacco raised in the colony, the people were outraged. In various places meetings were held to draw up a petition demanding redress. Some of Harvey's friends eavesdropping at a meeting held by Francis Pott, heard angry protests against the Governor's unjust and arbitrary government. When they reported this to Harvey, he had Pott and some of the others arrested, and threatened to try them by court martial.

But now he had gone too far. At a meeting of the Council he demanded the reasons for the circulating of the petition. When one of the Councillors said it was his detention of the Assembly's letter, Harvey struck him a resounding blow upon the shoulder, and blurted out: "Do you say so? I arrest you on suspicion of treason to his Majesty." At this point two other Councillors seized the Governor, crying, "And we you upon suspicion of treason to his Majesty." Then, at a signal about forty musketeers, who had been concealed near the house, rushed up "with their pieces presented." Forcing the enraged Governor into a chair, the Councillors poured out the recital of the people's wrongs. The only way they could save him from their fury was for him to leave the colony.

Harvey at first refused, but when he heard that the people were arming to bring him to account for his misdeeds, he changed his mind. However, he plucked up courage enough before he left to order an Assembly which was meeting without his summons, to disperse. Instead of doing so, they drew up resolutions charging him with misgovernment, and justifying his expulsion. It would have been well had they and the Council held the Governor in Virginia until their complaints had reached the King. As it was, Harvey, as soon as he landed at Plymouth, had their agents arrested, and seized all their papers. Apparently the King never received the Assembly's resolutions, and they are not to be found among the British records.

So Charles sent Harvey back. In January, 1637, in defiance of the threat that "if ever he returned back thither he would be pistoled or shot," he was back in Jamestown. And not only did he take ample revenge on his enemies, but began an odious tyranny, marked by confiscation, whippings, and "cutting of ears." But in the meanwhile charges against him began to pile up before the Privy Council, so that in 1639 that body removed him and appointed Sir Francis Wyatt in his place. The new Governor lost no time in bringing Harvey to account for his crimes, and forcing him to restore to their owners the estates he had confiscated for his own use.

The expulsion of Harvey is an important milestone in the development of self-government in both Virginia and England. Had Charles I, instead of upholding his tyrannical Governor, taken his expulsion as a proof that Englishmen, whether in England or America, would not submit to the loss of their liberty, there might have been no Civil War. In Virginia it gave warning to future Governors that it was dangerous to defy the Council and the Assembly, disregard the law, and trample on the people's rights. Certain Governors, in the years to come tried to build up despotic power by more subtle means, especially by the use of the patronage, but none dared to ride roughshod over the constitution.

Wyatt had been Governor only two years when he was replaced by Sir William Berkeley. During his first administration which covered the decade from 1642 to 1652, the new Governor ruled wisely and justly. He refused to persecute those implicated in the expulsion of Harvey, he tried to substitute an "income tax" for the levy by poll, he signed a bill to prohibit taxation by the Governor and Council, another exempting Burgesses from arrest during sessions of the Assembly, and still another fixing the fees of the Secretary of State. We need no further evidence that the people were happy and satisfied under his rule than his election by the Assembly to be Governor again at the moment when the Commonwealth was tottering to its fall.

Berkeley went to England at the outbreak of the Civil War and for some months fought with the royal forces before returning to Virginia; after the execution of Charles I he proclaimed Charles II King, and he surrendered Virginia to a Parliamentary expedition only when he found resistance hopeless. It was with bitterness that he handed over the reins of government to the Parliamentary commissioners and sat by as they transformed Virginia into a semi-independent republic.

The articles of surrender were liberal. The colony acknowledged its allegiance to the Commonwealth of England, and in return they were to have free trade with all nations. And they were "to be free from all taxes, customs, and impositions," except by the consent of the Grand Assembly. After these terms had been agreed to, the commissioners called for the election of a new Assembly, and when the members met, sat with them in what was in reality a constitutional convention.

The House of Burgesses was made the chief governing body of the colony, with powers unlimited except for a veto by the English government. They were to elect the Governor, determine his duties, and remove him from office if he proved unsatisfactory. They were to name the members of the Council and prescribe their functions. They took from the Governor the power of patronage, for it was agreed that all appointments to office were to belong "to the Burgesses, the representatives of the people."

Since the articles of surrender could not cover every detail of the new government, some of the subsequent acts of Assembly took on the character of constitutional amendments. In 1656 it was voted that "whereas we conceive it something hard and unagreeable to reason that any person shall pay equal taxes and yet have no votes in election . . . so much of the act for choosing Burgesses be repealed as excludes freemen from votes." The Assembly appointed the commander-in-chief of the militia; they regulated both the county courts and the General Court; they fixed the fees of the Secretary, county clerks, and sheriffs; they regulated foreign commerce.

Though it was stated that the Governor should have all the power formerly belonging to the office, it soon became obvious that this was not to be taken seriously. When the Governor and Council tried to dissolve the Assembly of 1658, they met with a rebuff. "The said dissolution, as the case standeth is not presidential, neither legal according to the laws," the Burgesses replied. In order to vindicate their authority they declared the "power of the government to reside in such persons as shall be impowered by the Burgesses, the representatives of the people, who are not dissolvable by any power now extant in Virginia." They then proceeded to "recall" the Governor and the Councillors, and hold a new election.

The Commonwealth Period in Virginia is notable for the training it gave the people and their representatives in self-government. For eight years they were free from the restraining hand of the King. There had been no English Governor set over them to veto their bills, sway the courts, bribe the Burgesses, and overawe the Council. Cromwell had promised to correct the "unsettledness" in the colony caused by "the looseness of the government," but he died before he could do so.

In the spring of 1660 the Assembly elected Sir William Berkeley Governor, and soon after, with the restoration of the monarchy, he received a commission from Charles II. But he was now a changed man. The experience of the Civil War had turned him into a bitter enemy of liberal institutions, so that he was determined that during his second administration there should be no more self-government in Virginia than his instructions required.

Berkeley's methods were more subtle than those of Sir John Harvey. Instead of overriding the Council and the Assembly, and browbeating the courts, he tried to win them over by a skilful use of the patronage. And when he had secured a House of Burgesses who were submissive to his will, he refused to dismiss them, but kept them on for many years.

Hartwell, Blair and Chilton, in their *Present State of Virginia*, go into considerable detail in explaining just how a Governor might fortify his power. "The Governor has . . . many ways to make an interest in the House of Burgesses . . . for first by means of the Council who are the commanders-in-chief of the several counties, and of other officers of the militia, who are either named by him or by the commanders-in-chief, he has a great stroke in the election of Burgesses for the Assembly. . . . The justices, who have great interest in every county, are commissioned by him during his pleasure." The sheriff, who enjoys "a good profitable place by his gift," is "always his fast friend." "The sheriff's place, being granted anew every year, is a constant fresh temptation to a great many pretenders to exert their utmost skill and interest in managing the election of the Burgesses of their several counties for the Governor. Then after these two Burgesses are actually chosen, one of them is very apt to be gained by the hopes of this same sheriff's place next year; or if either of them is a bold man in the House of Burgesses, the appointing him sheriff takes him out of the House. . . . By this art the Governor can either oblige and gain one of the two Burgesses of a county, or at least lay him aside, that he can do him no hurt."

If we may believe the accusations of the people of Charles City in response to the request of the King's commissioners to state their grievances after Bacon's Rebellion, Berkeley was a master of this art. "The said Sir William Berkeley, minding and aspiring to a sole and absolute power over us . . . greatly neglecting . . . the Council . . . did take upon him the sole naming and appointing of other persons in their room and place such as himself best liked and thought fittest for his purposes." He had also "assumed to himself the sole nominating, appointing, and commissioning of all commission officers both civil and military . . . and also offices of profit, which said offices being by the said Sir William Berkeley, the better to increase the number of his party, multiplied to a great number . . . all which offices he bestowed on such persons, how unfit or unskilful soever, as he conceived would be most for his designs. Having by these ways and means, by taking upon him contrary to law the granting collectors' places, sheriffs, and other offices of profit to whom he best pleased, he so gained upon and obliged all or the greatest number of men of parts and estates . . . [and] thereby so fortified his power over us as of himself without respect to our laws to do whatsover he best pleased."

Bacon declared that Berkeley "by his folly and passion together, hath involved himself and this poor colony in such a labyrinth of ruin . . . that he never can answer what he hath done before his Majesty. . . . All his damnable plots and devices against the people . . . his artifices, lies, and juggles must of necessity turn on himself." In his Manifesto Bacon said: "If there be, as sure there is, a just God to appeal to, . . . if to plead the cause of the oppressed, if sincerely to aim at his Majesty's honor and the public good . . . be treason, God Almighty judge and let [the] guilty die. . . . All the power and sway is got into the hands of the rich, who by extortious advantages, having the common people in their debt, have curbed and oppressed them in all manner of ways. . . . See what sponges have sucked up the public treasure and whether it has not been contrived away by unworthy favorites." The perpetual breach of laws, remiss prosecutions, excuses and evasions, but too plainly showed that things were carried by the men at the helm, "as if it were but to play a booty, game, or divide a spoil."

These "French despotic methods," as Richard Lawrence called them, were one of the principal causes of Bacon's Rebellion. The people at this time were no more willing to submit to arbitrary government than they had been under Harvey. But there were also other causes—the heavy taxes, the low price of tobacco, the granting to royal favorites of a large part of the colony, the two Dutch wars, a disastrous hurricane, and widespread poverty. When these misfortunes had laid the powder train, a bloody Indian war set off the explosion.

When the frontiersmen gathered in arms to defend their families from the murderous raids of the Indians and elected young Nathaniel Bacon their leader, they "vented their discontents in complaints of other grievances, also, too great to be wholly smothered." Bacon himself sent messengers to all parts of the country denouncing the Governor, complaining of the long continuance of the Assembly, and the restricting of the franchise. Berkeley stated that "by his emissaries" the people were induced to cry down "Assemblies not chosen by the people, but by a few men, as they said, of my faction." The Council wrote the Lords of Trade that Bacon had sent papers about the country "trying to traduce the Governor with many false and scandalous charges." In another letter they said he "has never ceased to load him with all the base calumnies and scandals . . . as all the black devils in hell could tempt him to." To Berkeley himself Bacon wrote that his men "in all their discourses," spoke of his falsehood, cowardice, treachery, receiving of bribes.

With hundreds of angry men in arms, and the whole country ready to rise, the Council urged the Governor to try to appease them by dissolving the old Assembly, and calling for an election in which all freemen had the right to vote. Reluctantly Berkeley complied. And he was alarmed when the returns came in showing all but eight of the new Burgesses to be of Bacon's "faction." Bacon, himself, was elected to represent Henrico. But when he came to Jamestown to take his seat, he was arrested, forced to make an humble submission, and then was restored to his place in the Council where Berkeley could watch him.

Thus deprived of their leader the pro-Bacon majority seem to have been afraid to defy the old Governor. Thomas Mathews, a member from Stafford, tells us that when "some gentlemen took this opportunity to endeavor the redressing several grievances the county then labored under," Berkeley sent pressing messages "to meddle with nothing until the Indian business was dispatched." When a resolution was introduced to ask Berkeley not to resign, they did not have the backbone to vote it down. To Bacon, who was a helpless witness of what was going on, it seemed that they had betrayed their trust.

Then suddenly all was changed; Bacon escaped and placed himself once more at the head of his army. This emboldened the Burgesses; it struck terror into the Governor and his supporters. "I did almost with tears beg of the Assembly to have one hundred volunteer gentlemen to be my guard; for the rabble I durst not trust, which was scornfully and peremptorily denied me," Berkeley said. When it was learned that Bacon and his men were marching on Jamestown, threatening to burn and ruin all, a series of reform bills were rushed through the Assembly and signed by the Governor in a last minute effort at appeasement.

On entering the town Bacon mounted the steps of the statehouse to the room where the Burgesses were sitting, and, unaware of what had happened during his absence, "pressed hard, nigh half an hour's harangue, on the preserving our lives from the Indians, inspecting the public revenue, the exorbitant taxes, and reducing the grievances and calamities of that deplorable country." "The Assembly told him they had taken care for the war ... and that they had redressed all their complaints." After the suppression of the rebellion, a newly elected Assembly declared all the acts of this Assembly void, because Bacon had threatened death to the Governor, Council, and Burgesses "if they would not grant his unreasonable, unlawful, rebellious, and treasonable demands." But though the reform laws were thus repealed, they are of great importance in the development of self-government in Virginia. They extended the right to vote to all freemen; they gave the people a voice in assessing county taxes; they put an end to self-perpetuating vestries; they fixed the fees of officials; sheriffs were to serve for one year only; Councillors were barred from sitting in the county courts; no person was to hold two of the offices of sheriff, clerk of the court, surveyor, or escheator at the same time. The passage of these laws is in itself evidence of the abuses they were designed to correct. They were obviously aimed at Berkeley's policy of rule through placemen, and he certainly would have refused to affix his signature had he not been under the pressure of Bacon's armed forces.

Bacon died in the midst of his battles, the rebellion collapsed, Bacon's chief supporters were sent to the gallows by the brutal old Governor, English troops were at hand to prevent any new uprising. But Berkeley did not long survive to dominate the colony by the old methods. King Charles sent for him to return to England, and on the way over he became ill. He died soon after landing.

There is no evidence that the despotism of Berkeley was a reflection of the spirit of the Restoration. It is true that the Governor, in keeping the Long Assembly for so many years, followed the example of Charles II in holding on to the Cavalier Parliament. But Charles had vowed that he would not resume his travels by driving the English people into a new rebellion, and this should have been a warning to Berkeley. Yet Sir William, though no pressure was brought on him by the King to curb representative government in the colony, succeeded in making himself virtually absolute.

In the decade which followed, the danger came, not so much from the Governors, but from England. The people of Virginia must have been alarmed when news came that King Charles had thrown aside his former caution and had entered upon a course of repression. He was attempting to rule without Parliament, his chief opponents were prosecuted in the courts, London and other cities were forced to give up their charters and accept new ones limiting the right to vote, Lord Russell and Algernon Sidney were executed, Shaftesbury fled to Holland. Later it came out that the King had accepted a large sum of money from Louis XIV, and with his pockets bulging had set out to make himself absolute. So began the Second Stuart Despotism.

Representative government continued at a low ebb under James II. This stubborn King was a Roman Catholic, who regarded it as his sacred duty to force his religion on the English people. He began by prosecuting Protestant dissenters, but soon changed to a policy of toleration for Protestants and Catholics alike. He filled many important posts in the government with Catholics, and tried to turn the universities into Catholic seminaries. It was only with the invasion of England by William of Orange and James' flight that these efforts came to an end.

The new despotism was felt immediately in the colonies. It was at this time that the King forced the Virginia Assembly to grant the Crown a perpetual revenue; it was at this time that he deprived the Assembly of its right to act as the supreme court of the colony. Though successful in these two measures, he failed in certain other assaults upon the liberties of the people.

In 1682 Charles tried to take over the disposal of all the revenues raised in the colony. The Assembly might specify the uses to which they wished funds to be placed, he said, but the money could not be paid until he had given his consent. But here he overreached himself. The disbursing of funds for salaries, or forts, or the fitting out of expeditions could not wait the sailing of some vessel for England, the long voyage over, the granting of the royal approval, and the return of some vessel to Virginia. So the order was quietly ignored, and the Assembly continued to pass revenue laws just as formerly.

It was distance and time which also nullified the King's instruction to Governor Culpeper that "for the future no General Assembly be called" without his special permission. There were no Atlantic cables over which the Governor could talk with Secretary Coventry to explain why it was necessary to call an Assembly and get his consent. He knew that if he wrote, it would be months, perhaps a year, before he could receive a reply. So this instruction, too, had to be ignored.

Equally unsuccessful was Charles' attempt to deprive the House of Burgesses of its right to initiate legislation. "You shall . . . transmit unto us, with the advice and consent of the Council, a draught of such acts as you shall think fit and necessary to be passed," he told Culpeper, "that we may take the same into our consideration and return them in the form we shall think they be enacted into." Then, and then only, were they to be placed before the Assembly for their approval. Culpeper must have seen at once that this would have made a mockery of representative government in Virginia. Moreover, it was quite impractical, for it would have made it necessary to delay important legislation for many months, perhaps for years.

In 1683 Culpeper was recalled and Lord Howard of Effingham made Governor General in his place. This boded ill for Virginia, for this man was well suited for carrying out the despotic designs of his royal master. Had it not been for the stiffest resistance by the Burgesses he might well have succeeded in reducing the Assembly to a rubber stamp.

It was under Effingham that the Assembly was deprived of its right to hear appeals from the lower courts. When the Burgesses heard that the King had given orders that they should no longer sit as a court, they begged the Governor to join them in an address imploring him to restore this privilege which they had enjoyed so long. But they met with a stern rebuke. "It is what I can in no part admit of," Effingham replied. So from this date to the end of the colonial period the structure of justice was aristocratic rather than democratic. Future governors had reason to regret this change, for it made the General Court, comprized as it was of the Councillors, the last court of appeals, and added greatly to their growing influence.

This was followed by an order from the King that certain causes arising in the courts be referred to England for decision. Against this the Burgesses protested. It would be "grievous and ruinous," they said in a petition to his Majesty, and would involve delays and great expense. The reception of this petition shows the resentment of King James II at any manifestation of popular sentiment in the colonies. To the Governor he wrote: "Whereas . . . our Committee of Trade and Plantations . . . have received from some unknown persons a paper entitled 'An Address and Supplication of the General Assembly of Virginia' to the late King . . . which you have refused to recommend as being unfit . . . we cannot but approve of your proceedings . . . and we do further direct you to discountenance such undue practices for the future, as also the contrivers and promoters thereof."

At this dark moment, when American liberty hung in the balance, the Burgesses were quick to repel any attempt to tax the people without their consent. In 1688 they stated that they had received many "grievous complaints" of the charging of unlawful fees, especially of a fee of 200 pounds of tobacco for affixing the great seal of the colony. And they were adamant in refusing to give permission for the Governor and Council by themselves to levy even the smallest tax.

In 1684 the King made an effort to build up the revenues

which were independent of the Burgesses, by ordering Effingham to accept payments of quit rents only in specie. In 1662 the Assembly had fixed the rate of payment at 2d a pound, payable in tobacco. Since in 1684 tobacco was selling at a half penny a pound the King's order would have quadrupled the value of the quit rents, imposed a heavy burden on the impoverished country, and strengthened the authority of the Crown.

When the Assembly refused to repeal the law of 1662, James voided it by proclamation. But the Burgesses "rudely and boldly disputed the King's authority in repealing laws by proclamation." Moreover, they pointed out that it was impossible to pay in specie since there were not enough coins in the entire colony. In the end the Governor was forced to assent to a compromise by which the quit rents were to be paid in tobacco at the rate of a penny per pound.

When James revived a law of 1680 concerning attorneys by voiding the repealing act of 1682, the Burgesses protested. "A law may as well receive its beginning by proclamation as such a revival," they said. They must have been startled when Effingham told them that the King had the right to nullify or revive what laws he pleased, since the only authority the Assembly had to legislate at all rested on a grant from the Throne. They had been under the impression that the right of the people to make laws through their representatives was inherent in all Englishmen. In an address to the Governor they stated that it was not for them to say what was or was not prerogative, but they made it clear that when it was stretched so far as to threaten the liberty of the people they would resist by every means in their power.

It was in keeping with the spirit of the Second Stuart Despotism that Charles and James would allow no press in Virginia. When John Buckner, a member of the House of Burgesses, employed a certain William Nuthead to set up a press at Jamestown, the latter was summoned before the Council to "answer for his presumption." The Council ordered that "for the prevention of all troubles and inconveniences that may be occasioned through the liberty of a press ... Mr. John Buckner and William Nuthead the printer enter into bond for £100" that they print nothing more until the pleasure of the King be known.

As Berkeley had used the patronage to fortify his own power, Effingham used it to force obedience to the King. William Sherwood and Colonel Thomas Milner were dismissed from office for forwarding an address of the Burgesses to the King; Mr. Arthur Allen was "turned out of all employment, civil and military," to his great loss, because he was a promoter of the differences between the Governor and the Assembly concerning the King's negative voice. Mr. Charles Scarburgh was "turned out of all employment, and, as a mark of his Lordship's displeasure, a command was sent to the clerk of the county to raze his name out of the records as a justice of the peace." Another Burgess, after the close of the session of 1688, was "put in the common jail" where he was kept seven months without trial. "From whence the people conclude these severities are inflicted rather as a terror to others than for any personal crimes of their own, and is of such ruinous consequence that either the public or particular interests must fall, for if none oppose, the country must languish under the severity of the government or fly into mutiny ... it being observable that none has been thus punished but those who were forward in the Assembly to oppose the encroachments on the people."

The people of Virginia feared that James might try to force Catholicism upon them. It was noticed that when important offices became vacant Effingham filled them with Catholics. He made only two appointments to the Council,—Colonel Isaac Allerton and Colonel John Armistead—both members of that Church. There were many in the colony who favored the Duke of Monmouth as King, and when news came that he had risen against James, they were open in their sympathy. Effingham re-

ported that "so many took liberty of speech upon the rebellion
... that I was fearful it would have produced the same here."

In fact, the people were ready to take up arms at the least excuse. A wild rumor was spread that the Papists had conspired with certain Indian tribes to cut off all the Protestants. In terror the outlying planters deserted their homes and fled with their families to the older settlements. Armed forces began to gather. It is possible that the movement was stimulated by the news that William of Orange was preparing to invade England. Effingham had left for England, but the Council took steps to suppress the uprising and punish some of the leaders. Then came the joyous word that William and Mary had been declared joint monarchs of England. At eleven in the morning of April 26, 1689, they were proclaimed before the door of the courthouse at Jamestown, to the firing of the great guns, the sounding of trumpets, the beating of drums, and the shouts of the crowd. The Second Stuart Despotism in Virginia was at an end.

The people of the colony were fully aware that the Glorious Revolution had initiated a new epoch of liberty. In an address to William and Mary the Assembly thanked them for "so magnanimously exposing" their persons in rescuing them, their religion, laws, and liberties. They begged their Majesties, while extending their justice and goodness over the English nation, not to forget their faithful subjects in Virginia. They, too, were "descended from Englishmen" and had the right to enjoy the liberties and privileges of freeborn Englishmen.

In this they were not disappointed. During the next seventy-five years the people advanced along the road to liberty with giant strides. From time to time they had to contend with reactionary Governors, who put the King's prerogative above the interests of the colony. But the Assembly was ever ready to defend old rights, ever ready to claim new privileges. By the middle of the eighteenth century the colony had become in internal affairs a self-governing dominion.

Francis Nicholson, who became Lieutenant-Governor by appointment of William and Mary, was by nature violent and arbitrary. But during his first term he so far suppressed his true character as to give the colony a just and progressive administration. He established cordial relations with both the Council and the House of Burgesses; he built up the defenses of the colony and put the militia in good order; he gave his hearty support to the founding of the College of William and Mary; he was solicitous for the welfare of the clergy.

The Assembly took advantage of the changed attitude of the English government to solicit a new charter, and appointed Jeffrey Jeffreys as their agent to press it. It was to contain provisions confirming the authority of the Assembly; promising "that no tax be made upon this country without the consent of the Assembly"; guaranteeing to the people the rights and privileges of natural born subjects of the realm of England; providing that "as near as may be" they should be governed after the same method as Englishmen; giving them the benefit of the Great Charter and all other laws concerning the liberty of the subjects. Although the Virginians did not secure the charter, it is important to know what they wished its provisions to be, and what they considered essential to the preservation of their liberty.

It must have been with apprehension that the people of Virginia heard that Sir Edmund Andros had been appointed Governor General, for the report of his despotism in New England had preceded him. They knew that there he had ruled like an Eastern despot, promulgating laws, levying taxes without the consent of the Assemblies, placing men under arrest and denying them the right of habeas corpus. And they were ready to offer stiff resistance should he try to rule Virginia with a harsh hand.

So they were surprised to find Andros a mild-mannered man, who not only made no assaults on their liberty, but tried to live

Office of Secretary of Colony, in which public records were preserved

Colonial Williamsburg Photo

Magazine and Guardhouse, Williamsburg, Virginia; the General Assembly passed the Act for its construction in 1714.

in peace with both Council and Burgesses. He seems not to have used the patronage to build up his power, he did not try to break the grip of the House on the purse by demanding large fees, he kept off the explosive subject of the arrears of quit rents. Edward Randolph whom the English government had sent over to investigate conditions in the colonies, said that he had "mightily gained upon the Council and the chief men in the country by his even temper." Obviously in New England he was reflecting the spirit of the Second Stuart Despotism; in Virginia he reflected the spirit of the Glorious Revolution.

Nothing can illustrate better the progress made in self-government in Virginia since the overthrow of James II than the cavalier treatment by the Burgesses of two bills recommended by the King and Queen. The first, a bill to prohibit the exportation of unpacked tobacco, was desired by the English merchants. The other, a bill to establish ports on the Virginia rivers, had been passed in 1688 and was now returned for certain revisions. The Burgesses promptly voted down both measures. Andros was much concerned at this disregard of the royal wishes, but when the Council advised him that nothing could be done with the Burgesses, he let the matter drop. Edward Randolph thought that this victory of the House boded no good. "They are full of conceit, and fancy themselves as great as the House of Commons in England," he said in disgust.

It was their "conceit" which made them insist upon controlling the expenditure of all funds raised by taxes they had voted. It had been the practice for the collectors to pay the money to the auditor, who appropriated it by the Governor's warrant to such uses as the Assembly had specified. But in 1691 the House claimed the "privilege of naming a treasurer for all money raised by themselves, without putting it in the auditor's hands, and that the treasurer should pay it away by their immediate orders, without any further warrant from the Governor." So in passing the act for the poll tax and an act levying a duty on liquors, they named Colonel Edward Hill as treasurer, and ordered that the revenue be paid him.

Nicholson countered by appointing Hill to a lucrative job as collector, which forced him to vacate the office, and then named Henry Whiting as treasurer. When the Burgesses passed a bill to supersede Whiting by a treasurer of their own selection the Council refused to concur. "The Governor would never consent to the Assembly's appointing their own treasurer but would rather lose a tax than suffer them to do so", James Blair testified later. But he added: "This makes them suspicious and more unwilling to raise money."

Whiting continued to hold the treasurership until his death in 1694. Then for several years there seems to have been no treasurer. But the Burgesses were merely biding their time, and their opportunity came in 1699. The old capitol at Jamestown had burned down, and there was urgent need to build a new one. So the Burgesses passed a bill placing a duty on the importation of servants and slaves, and a levy by poll, the revenue from both to be paid into the hands of the treasurer for this purpose. Since there was no treasurer they included in the act the appointment of Colonel Robert Carter to that office. The Governor and Council, realizing that they could not have the capitol without the treasurer, yielded.

The closing decade of the seventeenth century found Virginia well advanced on the road that led to liberty and independence. It is true that the Council had acquired great power, power which it used often for its own ends rather than the good of the people. But the Councillors, with rare exceptions, were native Virginians, and as such opposed, at times openly, at other times subtly, measures harmful to the colony. Moreover, as time passed, they were more and more overshadowed by the growing power of the Burgesses.

The English government was warned of what was coming.

In 1706, Colonel Robert Quarry wrote: "I may truly say that now or never is the only time to maintain the Queen's just prerogative, and put a stop to these wrong, pernicious notions which are improving daily, not only in Virginia, but in all Her Majesty's other governments. A frown now from Her Majesty will do more than perhaps an army hereafter."

Time proved that Quarry was right. At the accession of George III the people of English colonies on the continent of North America were the freest in the world. The power of the royal Governors had been reduced to a minimum, the great middle class, well-to-do and contented, ruled the colonies through the medium of the Lower Houses. In their protests against the Stamp Act the Americans described themselves as a free people, and expressed their determination to maintain their rights and liberties.

But it should not be forgotten that the rights and liberties of the time of Washingon, Jefferson, Mason, and Henry were based on the hard fought battles of the seventeenth century. It should not be forgotten that in Virginia the people's representatives again and again braved the King's anger to defend their rights, that they repeatedly defied his Governors, that they insisted upon having all the privileges of Englishmen, that they had to contend with the brutal cruelty of a Dale, the despotism of a Harvey, the arbitrariness of a Berkeley, the avarice of a Culpeper, that they upheld the banner of liberty through the despotisms of Charles I, Charles II, and James II, that the people expelled one Governor and rose in rebellion against another.

The spirit which animated the early Virginians is shown in a statement of Philip Ludwell, Jr.: "That which bears up their spirits . . . is that they have the happiness to enjoy the English laws and constitution, which they reckon the best of governments. But if once their Governors be suffered to break in upon them in this tender point . . . it is not to be imagined how ill this will go down with Englishmen that have not forgot the liberty of their mother country." It was this spirit which animated Bacon's ragged rebels; and it was this spirit which, exactly a century later, led to the Revolution and independence.

ESSAY ON AUTHORITIES.

Source material for the government of Virginia under the London Company is relatively abundant. Of first importance is Susan M. Kingsbury's edition of *The Records of the Virginia Company of London*, which brings together many of the documents relating to the first years of the colony. W. W. Hening, in his *The Statutes at Large*, publishes the early laws, charters, and various articles, instructions, and orders. The deaf historian, Alexander Brown, has collected many important documents throwing new light on the period, which he published in his *The Genesis of the United States*. Brown's *The First Republic in America* is also a great help to historians. The *Travels and works of Captain John Smith*, edited by Edward Arber and A. G. Bradley is indispensable, as is Peter Force's *Tracts and Other Papers*. One finds, also, much material in The *William and Mary Quarterly*, and *Tyler's Magazine*. Among the secondary sources are Wesley Frank Craven's *Dissolution of the Virginia Company*, Philip Alexander Bruce's *Institutional History of Virginia in the Seventeenth Century*, Matthew Page Andrews' *Virginia, the Old Dominion*, and Charles M. Andrews' *Colonial Period of American History*.

The materials for Virginia history during the reign of Charles I are meager. But one finds in the British Public Record Office documents and correspondence sufficient to reconstruct with some degree of accuracy the course of events leading to the expulsion of Sir John Harvey. Our chief reliance, however is on Hening's *Statutes*. Here one finds the acts passed by the Assembly, the names of Councillors and Burgesses, and other valuable papers. Unfortunately, there is little in the Public Record Office to throw light on Sir William Berkeley's first administration. But much can be gleaned from such county records as have survived the destruction of fire and wars. One finds, also, occasionally a document published in one of the historical magazines. Among the secondary sources are T. J. Wertenbaker, *Virginia Under the Stuarts*, P. A. Bruce, *Institutional History of Virginia*, Robert Beverley, *The History and Present State of Virginia*.

For the Commonwealth period the sources are even more meager. There was little or no correspondence between the Virginia officials and the English government, so one searches in vain in the Public Record Office for clues as to what was going on in the colony. The historian has to fall back again on Hening and the county records. This period must always remain obscure unless we stumble upon new mines of information.

We have far more information concerning the Restoration period. In the Public Record Office are several manuscript volumes filled with letters from Berkeley, Thomas Ludwell, Sir Henry Chicheley, and others; with the transactions of the Virginia agents; with reports, petitions, etc. These are supplemented by Hening's *Statutes,* the county records, and many papers published in the *Virginia Magazine* and other historical magazines. Of events leading up to and during Bacon's Rebellion there are numerous accounts—the *True Narrative,* of the King's commissioners; Thomas Mathews' *The Beginning, Progress and Conclusion of Bacon's Rebellion;* Mrs. Ann Cotton's *Bacon's Proceedings* and *Ingram's Proceedings,* etc. There are many other documents which throw light on the rebellion—for example: "The Memorial of John Knight," Chicheley's commission as Governor, and Thomas Bacon's petition to the King.

The Marquess of Bath Papers, recently opened to historians, throw a flood of light on Bacon's Rebellion. Especially valuable is the correspondence between Bacon and Berkeley, Philip Ludwell's letters to Lady Berkeley and to Thomas Ludwell, Berkeley's explanations of why he called a new Assembly, why he pardoned Bacon, and why he evacuated Jamestown, etc., and the Council's account of Bacon's Occaneechee campaign. The papers reveal the timidity of the Assembly of June 1676 while Bacon was virtually a prisoner, and their boldness in defying the Governor and pushing through reform laws after he had made his escape and was leading his army down on Jamestown.

Among the secondary sources on Bacon's Rebellion are T. J. Wertenbaker, *Torchbearer of the Revolution* and *Virginia Under the Stuarts;* Mary Newton Stanard, *The Story of Bacon's Rebellion;* P. A. Bruce, *Institutional History of Virginia;* Herbert L. Osgood, *The American Colonies in the Seventeenth Century;* Lyon G. Tyler, *The Cradle of the Republic;* and Wesley Frank Craven, *The Southern Colonies in the Seventeenth Century, 1607-1689.*

For the period of the Second Stuart Despotism, and for the decade following the Glorious Revolution there is abundant source material. The English government had given orders that copies of the journals of both the Council and the House of Burgesses be sent them, and these invaluable documents have been preserved and are now in the Public Record Office. They have since been published by the State of Virginia. But historians still rely on Hening's *Statutes* for the acts passed during this period. For the correspondence of Governors and other officials with the Lords of Trade, we must again turn to the British Public Record Office. But it is fortunate that the mass of papers in this office, covering scores of volumes, has been transcribed by the United States government, and is available to historians through inter-library loans. Much of the material is to be found in an abbreviated form in the *Calendar of State Papers, Colonial Series, America and West Indies, 1564-1736. The Executive Journals of the Council, The Legislative Journals of the Council,* and *The Journals of the House of Burgesses, 1619-1659, 1659-1693,* have been published. Fortunate is it, also, that the Virginia county records before 1861 have been microfilmed by the Utah Genealogical Society and deposited in the Virginia State Library.

One of the most illuminating sources for the history of the government of Virginia is Hartwell, Blair, and Chilton's *The Present State of Virginia*, written in 1697. It was first published in 1727, but in 1940 Hunter D. Farish was the editor of a new edition published by Colonial Williamsburg, Inc. Robert Beverley's *The History and Present State of Virginia*, though written later than the work of Hartwell, Blair, and Chilton, was published twenty-two years earlier. In 1947 a new edition appeared edited by Louis B. Wright. Both works devote much space to descriptions of the various offices of government, and though not free from bias, they have the freshness of contemporary evidence.

Unfortunately, although the materials are plentiful and have been made easily available, the period from the end of Bacon's Rebellion to the end of the century is the most neglected in Virginia history. Historians have written fully of the Second Stuart Despotism in New England, but have neglected the equally critical time in the Old Dominion.

Invaluable to students of early Virginia history is the *Virginia Historical Index*, by E. G. Swem, of *The Virginia Magazine of History*, 1893-1930; *William and Mary Quarterly*, 1892-1930; *Tyler's Magazine*, 1919-1929; *Virginia Historical Register*, 1848-1853; *Lower Norfolk County Antiquary*, 1895-1906; *Hening's Statutes at Large*, 1619-1792; *Calendar of Virginia State Papers*, 1652-1869.

www.ingramcontent.com/pod-product-compliance
Lightning Source LLC
Chambersburg PA
CBHW051948160426
43198CB00013B/2359